SandCastle™

Baby
Australian Animals

It's a Baby
Tasmanian
Devil!

Katherine Hengel

Consulting Editor, Diane Craig, M.A./Reading Specialist

ABDO
Publishing Company

Published by ABDO Publishing Company, 8000 West 78th Street, Edina, Minnesota 55439.

Copyright © 2010 by Abdo Consulting Group, Inc. International copyrights reserved in all countries.

No part of this book may be reproduced in any form without written permission from the publisher. SandCastle™ is a trademark and logo of ABDO Publishing Company.

Printed in the United States.

Editor: Liz Salzmann
Content Developer: Nancy Tuminelly
Cover and Interior Design and Production: Kelly Doudna, Mighty Media
Photo Credits: Geoffrey Lea/AUSCAPE, keiichihiki/iStockphoto.com,
BIOS Bios-Auteurs Watts Dave/Peter Arnold Inc.

Library of Congress Cataloging-in-Publication Data

Hengel, Katherine.
  It's a baby Tasmanian devil! / Katherine Hengel.
    p. cm. -- (Baby Australian animals)
  ISBN 978-1-60453-579-2
  1. Tasmanian devil--Infancy--Australia--Juvenile literature. I. Title.

QL737.M33H46 2010
599.2'7--dc22
                          2009003080

SandCastle™ Level: Fluent

SandCastle™ books are created by a team of professional educators, reading specialists, and content developers around five essential components—phonemic awareness, phonics, vocabulary, text comprehension, and fluency—to assist young readers as they develop reading skills and strategies and increase their general knowledge. All books are written, reviewed, and leveled for guided reading, early reading intervention, and Accelerated Reader® programs for use in shared, guided, and independent reading and writing activities to support a balanced approach to literacy instruction. The SandCastle™ series has four levels that correspond to early literacy development. The levels are provided to help teachers and parents select appropriate books for young readers.

Emerging Readers
(no flags)

Beginning Readers
(1 flag)

Transitional Readers
(2 flags)

Fluent Readers
(3 flags)

SandCastle™ would like to hear from you. Please send us your comments and suggestions.
sandcastle@abdopublishing.com

Vital Statistics

for the Tasmanian Devil

BABY NAME
joey

NUMBER IN LITTER
2 to 4

WEIGHT AT BIRTH
less than ⅟₁₀₀ ounce (¼ g)

AGE OF INDEPENDENCE
8 months

ADULT WEIGHT
9 to 26 pounds (4 to 12 kg)

LIFE EXPECTANCY
5 to 8 years

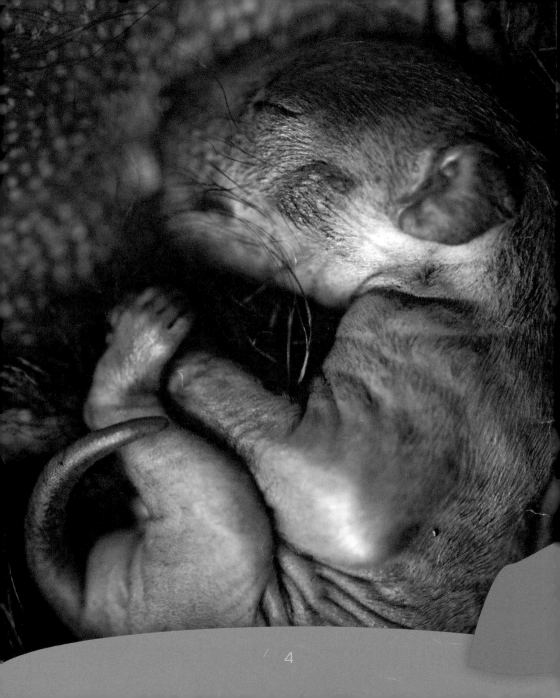

A newborn Tasmanian devil lives in its mother's pouch. It **nurses** all the time and grows quickly.

Joeys stay in the pouch for about four months.

After they leave the pouch, the joeys never go back inside it. They stay in the den with their mother.

The mother **protects** her joeys and shows them how to find food.

Tasmanian devils are nocturnal. They rest in their dens during the day and eat at night.

Tasmanian devils make their dens in **burrows**, caves, and hollow logs.

Tasmanian devils are **carnivores**. They **prey** on insects and small animals. They also eat animals that are already dead.

Tasmanian devils eat every part of an animal. Even the bones and fur!

Sometimes Tasmanian devils eat in groups. When they eat, they growl, **snarl**, and screech very loudly.

Tasmanian devils have a lot of long **whiskers**. Their whiskers help them sense **prey** and danger.

When Tasmanian devils are scared or excited, their ears turn red.

Eagles and **dingoes**
prey on Tasmanian devils.
Also, many Tasmanian
devils die from **cancer**.

Only Tasmanian devils get
a kind of cancer called
devil facial tumor disease.

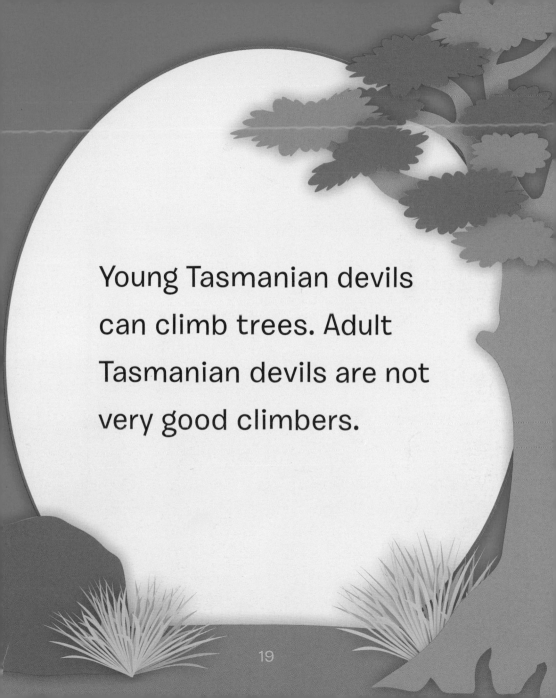

Young Tasmanian devils
can climb trees. Adult
Tasmanian devils are not
very good climbers.

A Tasmanian devil becomes independent when it is eight months old. It leaves the mother's den to live on its own.

Tasmanian devils **yawn** to show their teeth when they are afraid.

21

Fun Fact

About the Tasmanian Devil

When a Tasmanian devil is born, it is smaller than a raisin. When it leaves the pouch, it is almost as big as a grapefruit. That's about 2,000 times bigger!

Glossary

burrow – a hole or tunnel dug in the ground by a small animal for use as shelter.

cancer – a disease that causes some cells in the body to grow faster than normal and attack healthy organs and tissues.

carnivore – one who eats meat.

dingo – an Australian wild dog.

nurse – to drink milk from a mother's breast.

prey – 1) to hunt or catch an animal for food. 2) an animal that is hunted or caught for food.

protect – to guard someone or something from harm or danger.

snarl – to growl and show one's teeth.

whisker – one of the long hairs around the mouth of an animal.

yawn – to open one's mouth very wide and breathe deeply.

To see a complete list of SandCastle™ books and other nonfiction titles from ABDO Publishing Company, visit **www.abdopublishing.com**.
8000 West 78th Street, Edina, MN 55439
800-800-1312 • 952-831-1632 fax